Personal Brand Brilliance

Make Your Mark in the Digital Age

Table of Contents

Chapter 1. Introduction

Step into the vibrant and transforming world of digital personal branding with our Special Report, "Personal Brand Brilliance: Make Your Mark in the Digital Age." This report is your golden ticket to understanding and leveraging the power of personal branding like never before. We unlock the secrets of creating a standout online persona that truly resonates with your audience in this new era. Woven with engaging case studies, powerful insights, and practical strategies, this report is a must-have treasure for anyone aspiring to shine brightly in the digital landscape. Let's illuminate your path to personal brand brilliance - your radiant journey starts here!

Chapter 2. Unveiling the Power of Personal Branding

In an age where we are constantly interconnected through various digital platforms, the concept of personal branding has taken on an entirely new level of importance and potential. It's akin to a distinct signature that sets apart your persona, your values, and your unique selling proposition from the millions of voices on the internet.

Let's first deconstruct the fundamental elements of a wildly powerful personal brand.

2.1. Conceptualizing Your Personal Brand

Identifying your niche and understanding your target audience sets the foundation for an effective personal brand strategy. A niche within a broader industry that you are knowledgeable and passionate about is your ideal target. Answering questions like who are you trying to reach and what do they value can help you create a brand image that targets their needs and interests.

Throughout this process, take the time to share your journey authentically. Storytelling is a powerful tool in personal branding that can connect you with your audience on a deeper level and foster credibility and trust.

2.2. Building a Identifiable Brand Identity

An identifiable brand identity is the visual representation of the value you offer. This identity is expressed through your logo, colors, typography, and design elements. Consistency in these elements across all digital platforms helps to ensure that your audience can immediately recognize your brand, enhancing your visibility and recall value.

To create a memorable brand identity, leverage design thinking strategies such as empathy, iteration, and user testing. Effective design can powerfully communicate your brand story, values, and personality.

2.3. Optimizing Digital Presence

The digital landscape offers several avenues to maintain from professional networking platforms like LinkedIn to social media platforms like Instagram or Facebook. Being active across multiple platforms increases your visibility, engages your audience, and builds a strong online reputation.

High-quality, value-driven content is at heart of effective digital optimization. Whether through blog posts, social media updates, or e-books, consistently delivering useful content helps to position you as a thought leader in your field. Keep in mind; consistency is the key to building and maintaining an active digital presence.

2.4. Leveraging Social Proof

Testimonials, endorsements, and successful case studies serve as social proof, reinforcing your reputation as an industry expert. They offer third-party validation of your skills, knowledge, and expertise, building trust among your audience.

2.5. Networking and Collaboration

While having a stellar online presence is undeniable essential, do not underestimate the power of offline networking and collaboration. Cooperation with others within your industry can lead to opportunities for guest blogging, partnerships, and joint ventures. These efforts broaden your reach and exposure, providing a credible boost to your brand.

2.6. Measuring Success and Iterating Your Strategy

Lastly, tracking and measuring the success of your personal branding efforts is crucial. Analytics inform you about what's working and what needs improvement. Following measurement and analytics, you should iterate and refine your strategy based on data-driven insights.

Despite being a term often thrown around, personal branding is more than just a buzzword; it is the symbiotic relationship between success and identity in the digital world. Charting the course for a powerful personal brand can seem demanding initially; however, with meticulous planning, creative thinking, and consistent execution, your brand can truly resonate with your audience penetrating the digital noise. The future of personal branding is radiant with immense potential, and the power to unlock that potential is in your hands. Just remember, Rome wasn't built in a day, and neither will your brand be. A little patience, a lot of perseverance, and consistent efforts will soon let you shine brightly in the digital landscape.

Chapter 3. Transforming Pixels into Personality: Creating Your Digital Identity

Unearthing the essence of your personal brand begins with introspection. Understanding who you are, your values, experiences, skills, and aspirations forms the bedrock of your digital identity. Be prepared for self-discovery. The outcome? An online persona that is genuine, relatable, and distinctive.

3.1. Defining Your Personal Brand Core

Your personal brand core encapsulates your essence, distilling it into guiding principles. These principles should represent your values, beliefs, and aspirations, functioning as your brand's compass. For instance, if creativity is a cornerstone of your brand, it should reflect in every aspect of your digital identity from visual content, language style, to the topics you choose to discuss.

Similarly, your skills and experiences provide layers and depth to your branding. A tenured executive might emphasize leadership skills and industry expertise, while an up-and-coming professional might focus on innovative thinking or novel methodologies. Remember – uniqueness lies in your authentic experiences and perspective.

Start with defining your personal brand core:

- Identify your values - What guiding principles do you live or work by?

- Compile your skillset - What are your areas of professional expertise?

- Understand your aspirations - Where do you see your brand in the future?

- Catalog your experiences - What have you done that aligns with your brand?

The answers should form a blueprint of your digital personality.

3.2. Injecting Personality into Your Online Presence

A compelling digital identity requires personality, injected consistently across all platforms. Each interaction - be it a blog post, a tweet, a YouTube video - is a chance to show your audience the person behind the brand, bridging the virtual divide and creating real connections.

Here's how to infuse personality consistently:

- Set a Tone of Voice: Your tone should reflect your brand's personality, whether it's conversational, formal, or playful. Consistency creates familiarity, enticing audiences to engage more because they know what to expect.

- Choose Visuals Thoughtfully: Images, palettes, fonts, and logos should coordinate into a visual symphony that resonates your brand. If your brand is bold and edgy, vibrant colors and modern fonts might work best.

- Share Personal Anecdotes: Storytelling is a powerful tool. Sharing personal experiences or insights helps audiences relate to the person behind the brand image, fostering deep emotional connections.

3.3. Harnessing Social Media to Elevate Your Brand

Social media platforms are your stage, each offering unique ways to project your brand. Twitter's brevity might be ideal for sharing industry insights, LinkedIn for professional networking, and Instagram for visual storytelling. The key is to leverage the uniqueness of each platform to your brand's advantage while maintaining cross-platform consistency.

Consider the following when building your social media presence:

- Select the Right Platforms: Each platform appeals to a specific demography. Choose platforms where your target audience is most active.

- Craft Platform-Specific Content: Each platform has a unique content 'vibe'. LinkedIn is professional, Twitter is quick and witty, while Instagram is visually compelling. Tailor your content to fit these vibes.

- Engage Actively: Liking, sharing, and commenting—be active on your platforms. Engaging with your audience builds a sense of community, encouraging mutual interaction.

3.4. Consistency: The Crucial Ingredient

Consistency is queen in the realm of personal branding. It fortifies your brand, transforming it into a memorable, reliable presence in the digital sphere. Consistency encapsulates everything from visuals, tone of voice, posting frequency, to your brand's principles—the crux of your online personality.

Consider:

- Posting Frequency: Train your audience when to expect content. A regular schedule enables anticipation, driving engagement.

- Themes & Topics: Develop thematic consistency—audiences should know what type of content to expect from you. It also bolsters your reputation as an expert in your chosen niche.

- Visuals & Tone: Manage consistency in visuals and tone across all platforms.

3.5. Your Digital Identity: A Living, Breathing Entity

Remember, your digital identity isn't set in stone; it's a living, breathing entity that evolves with you. Regular reviews allow tweaks that reflect your personal growth, ensuring your brand remains authentic.

Creating a captivating digital identity might seem daunting—relax, take one step at a time. Think of it as an exploration; chart the terrain, map your journey. With every pixel representing a piece of you, a complete picture will emerge.

Chapter 4. The Art of Storytelling in Branding

The power of storytelling has been recognized since time immemorial. The same remains true in the digital age, only the medium has shifted from cave walls and scrolls to websites and social platforms. In the context of personal branding, storytelling has received a digital makeover yet it leverages the same timeless principles at its core.

4.1. Understanding the Role of Storytelling

First and foremost, it's essential to understand what storytelling is and the purpose it serves in personal branding. Simply put, storytelling in personal branding is the sum of your experiences, values, skills, and aspirations articulated in a compelling and relatable narrative. It is not a fictional tale but a unique interpretation of your journey and intentions that inspires, engages, and influences others.

We, humans, are wired to connect with stories. We tend to remember stories better than facts or data. When you spell out your journey in a story format, your audience is more likely to internalize it. It differentiates you from others, meaning it sets you apart and makes you memorable. It's your chance to humanize your personal brand by showing your vulnerabilities, wins, insights, and dreams. Most importantly, a well-crafted story can inspire people to take the action you desire them to.

4.2. Elements of a Powerful Personal Brand Story

A good brand story strikes a fine balance between who you are (your values and experiences) and what your audience cares about (their needs, dreams, and challenges). Here are some key elements to include in your personal brand story:

1. Your 'Why': The reason that drives you, the purpose behind your actions, your ultimate motivation.

2. Your Journey: Your experiences, accomplishments, and failures that shaped your current abilities and perspective.

3. Your Vision: A glance into the future, portraying where you intend to go and how you intend to make a difference.

4. Challenges: Your struggles and how you overcame them can make your story more relatable and inspiring.

5. Unique Value Proposition: What sets you apart from others in your niche.

6. Connection to the Audience: A clear depiction of how your story benefits your audience or resonates with their journey or aspirations.

4.3. Crafting Your Personal Brand Story

Now that we've understood the "why" and "what" of the personal brand story, let's delve into the "how." Crafting your personal brand story demands introspection, creativity, and authenticity. But rest assured, the efforts you put in will pay off handsomely in the form of an engaged and loyal audience.

1. Understand your audience: Your story needs to resonate with

your audience. So, understand their needs, concerns, aspirations, and values. This knowledge will guide you to craft a narrative that aligns with your audience.

2. Be Authentic: Authenticity lies at the heart of personal branding. Share real experiences and emotions, and don't shy away from including your vulnerabilities and failures. This authenticity helps you connect deeply with your audience.

3. Use Emotional Appeal: Emotions can be a powerful tool to engage your audience. Stirring positive emotions such as motivation, inspiration, empathy, or love in your audience can effectively form a deep emotional connection with them.

4. Keep It Simple and Relatable: Layman's language works best for storytelling. Your story must be easy to understand, relatable, and accessible. Restrict the use of jargon and complex words.

5. Evolve Your Story: As you grow and evolve, so should your story. Regularly updating your personal brand story keeps it relevant and relatable to your current audience.

4.4. Harnessing Digital Platforms for Storytelling

The digital age provides a vast array of platforms to communicate your personal brand story to your audience. Let's look at how you can effectively leverage them.

1. Websites and Blogs: Your personal website or blog is a great place to elaborate your story. Include your journey, vision, values, and key learnings on the 'About Me' page.

2. Social Media: Different platforms cater to different audiences. Adjust your storytelling style accordingly. For instance, Instagram is perfect for visual storytelling through photos, graphics, and short videos, while LinkedIn is suitable for professional and formal narratives.

3. Videos: If a picture is worth a thousand words, a video is worth a million. Platforms like YouTube offer an excellent opportunity for in-depth storytelling, be it through talking-head videos, animations, or documentaries.

4. Podcasts: If you're more comfortable speaking than writing, consider sharing your story through podcasts. Intimate and convenient, podcasts can help you create a strong personal connection with your audience.

5. E-books & PDFs: If you've got a long and detailed story to tell, consider creating an e-book or a downloadable PDF file. This format is perfect for delivering valuable content that your audience can consume at their own pace.

The art of storytelling in personal branding is both a science and an art. It involves understanding the principles of narrative, knowing the tastes and preferences of your audience, and weaving it all together with creativity and authenticity. With practice, anyone can master it and shine brightly in the personal branding universe. It's now your turn to take this knowledge, unravel your story, and let your personal brand starlight touch every corner of the digital universe.

Chapter 5. Harnessing Social Media for Brand Promotion

In the ever-evolving digital landscape, social media stands as a shining beacon of opportunity, a platform that promises infinite reach and boundless potential. Harnessing it for personal brand promotion is a surefire way to propel your brand into the spotlight. However, navigating social media requires astute understanding, smart strategies, and dedicated effort.

5.1. Understanding the Social Media Landscape

A firm ground understanding of the social media landscape is the first step in effectively utilizing it for personal brand promotion. Different social media platforms cater to different audiences and offer unique ways to deliver your brand's message. The choice of platform largely depends on factors like your target audience, the nature of your brand message, and your communication style.

Facebook, for example, is ideal for businesses seeking to forge an emotional bond with their audience. Instagram, with its visual-first format, is perfect for brands with strong visual elements or storytelling. LinkedIn helps create professional networks and is ideal for business-to-business brand promotion. Twitter excels at rapid dissemination of information and new ideas. TikTok and Snapchat, with their younger user base, are great for brands with a youthful, energetic vibe.

Thus, choosing the right platforms that align with your brand message and target audience is crucial.

5.2. Crafting a Compelling Online Persona

Simply understanding the social media landscape isn't enough. You must craft a compelling online persona that communicates who you are and what you stand for; this persona is your brand.

Start by introspecting about your core values, passions, strengths, and the unique value you provide. Carry forward these elements consistently across all your profiles. Maintain a unified visual theme using colors, images, and typography that capture your brand's essence. This consistency creates recognizable patterns, helping your audience easily identify and remember you.

5.3. Content is King

In the digital age, Content is indeed the king. It drives engagement, fosters relationships and ultimately, amplifies your personal brand.

A mix of valuable, relatable and engaging content should be the cornerstone of your strategy. While informational posts establish your expertise, motivational quotes and personal anecdotes foster a deeper emotional connection with your audience.

Interaction-driven content, such as live Q&As, webinars, or how-to videos, engages your audience and encourages them to be a part of your brand journey.

Lastly, maintain consistency in your posting schedule. The more consistent you are, the more familiar and reliable you become to your audience.

5.4. Engaging With Your Audience

Social media is not just a broadcast tool but also a platform for two-way communication. Engaging with your audience opens a dialog, builds relationships, and enriches your personal brand.

Respond to comments, appreciate shares, and reciprocate follows. Provide valuable responses to inquiries or criticisms. Actively participate in relevant group discussions. All these activities show your audience that you value their opinions and appreciate their involvement, thus cultivating a loyal community around your brand.

5.5. Leveraging Social Media Tools

Most social media platforms offer a variety of tools and features that can immensely help in promoting your personal brand. Live video streaming, Stories, Fleets, and Reels are just a few examples. Use these features to display different aspects of your brand personality and showcase behind-the-scenes moments.

Harness insights from social media analytics. These provide valuable data on what type of content your audience enjoys most, the best times to post, and how your content is performing. This helps you adjust your strategy for optimum reach and engagement.

5.6. Paid Promotions

Despite the benefits of organic growth, certain circumstances may warrant the use of paid promotions. Social media platforms offer sophisticated targeting options that let you reach a specific demographic with your ads or sponsored content.

Conduct A/B testing on your ads, evaluate their performance, and tweak your strategy to constantly improve your advertising effectiveness.

By understanding and properly utilizing the social media landscape, your personal brand can attain heights unimagined. Remember, social media is a journey, not a destination. Keep evolving, iterating, and improving your strategies as the landscape shifts. Your consistency, dedication, and imbibing the above strategies will eventually etch your strong social media presence, illuminating your personal brand brilliance in the digital age.

Chapter 6. Beyond Logos: Visual Aspects of Your Brand

In the realm of personal branding, few elements stand as critical and potentially as influential as our visual clues. These facets include but are not limited to our logos, color palettes, typefaces, and overall aesthetic design. All are potent components that contribute to an in-depth, meaningful, and, most significantly, recognizable brand identity.

6.1. The Lever of Visual Identity

The visual identity of a brand refers to how it appears and communicates visually to the public. This includes an assortment of visual devices and graphics, including logos, typography, colors, website layouts, social media graphics, business cards, and any other visuals that you use to portray your brand.

Let's break it down further and identify the key elements that compose a brand's visual identity:

1. **Logos:** The logo is often the first thing that comes to mind when considering a brand identity. It serves as the principal graphical representation of the brand, carrying the brand's voice, message, and philosophy.

2. **Color Palette:** The colors you choose for your brand are equally crucial. They can evoke certain emotions and create visual coherence across different platforms.

3. **Typography:** This refers to the fonts you choose. Different fonts carry different personalities and can directly influence how your message is perceived.

4. **Imagery and Graphics:** This considers the type of images and graphics commonly associated with your brand. A consistent

style of imagery strengthens brand recognition.

6.2. Digging Deeper into Logos

While logos hold immense power, we should not underestimate the contribution of other elements. Every logo, however sophisticated, still needs a strong brand palette to augment its impact. A sole focus on a logo is reductive - akin to serving the first course of a meal and eschewing the rest.

A logo aids in recognition but doesn't singlehandedly shoulder the brand's weight. It cannot express everything about your brand, nor should it. A brand is an amalgam of experiences and perceptions, much larger than any single visual element.

6.3. The Power of Color Palette

Colors hold an inherent psychological value. Various studies suggest that people make a subconscious judgment about an environment or product within 90 seconds of initial viewing, and 62%-90% of that assessment is based on color alone. Strategic color implementation can significantly impact a brand's message, increase brand recognition, and ultimately drive consumer engagement.

When selecting your brand's color palette, it's critical to consider colors that differentiate you from direct competitors and stand out within the social media landscape where your target audience spends time. It's about a harmonious blend that promotes visual coherence and reflects your brand's personality.

6.4. Typography: The Unsung Hero

Typography is often overlooked in light of more obvious branding components like the logo or color, but fonts play an enormous role in conveying your brand message. Serif fonts speak to tradition and reliability, while sans serif fonts suggest modernity and innovation. Script fonts carry an element of sophistication, while handwritten fonts can convey a sense of creativity or approachability.

Incorporate typography that aligns with your brand's persona and make it consistent across all platforms for an uninterrupted brand experience.

6.5. Harnessing Imagery and Graphics

An evolutionary trait hardwired in our brains is our ability to process visual data better than textual information. The rise of social media has seemingly magnified that trait with platforms centered around aesthetics and visuals.

Imagery and graphics are potent tools that complement your overall brand design. Using consistent visuals strengthens brand recall, tells your brand's story more effectively, and helps forge emotional connections with your audience.

Leverage high-quality and relevant images, infographics, diagrams, charts, and iconography that align with your brand. Be consistent in style, color, composition, tone, and emotion.

This comprehensive understanding of the visual aspects of branding is where many often miss a trick, focusing too narrowly on logos. But to truly crack the code of personal branding, one needs to grasp the interplay of all these different aspects. As we pave your path to personal brand brilliance, let's ensure you give each of these visual aspects its due, creating a visually cohesive and compelling brand.

After all, personal branding is much more than a logo; it's about creating a visual language that communicates your identity, your values, and your promise to your audience. In doing so, you'll achieve a level of recognition and resonance that goes well beyond the surface, striking a chord with your audience on a deeper, more meaningful level.

Chapter 7. Mastering the Science of SEO for Personal Branding

SEO, or Search Engine Optimization, forms the bedrock of any effective digital strategy. It's a method to increase the visibility of your digital persona on various search engines. By tweaking certain aspects of your online presence, you can ensure that you're easily discovered by those looking for the unique value you provide.

7.1. Understanding the Basics of SEO

The rudimentary element to understand about SEO is how search engines operate. Programs called spiders are dispatched by search engines like Google, Bing, or Yahoo to crawl the Web, indexing or organizing sites based on various factors, such as content relevance. Search engines use algorithms to decide how useful a site is to a user's query and rank it accordingly in the search results.

The aim is to appear on the first page of the search results—for that's where the majority of clicks are. This determines your online visibility, and by extension, the reach and strength of your personal brand.

7.2. Keyword Research and Optimization

Keyword research forms the foundation stone of SEO. These "keywords" are what users are likely to type into search engines when looking for the content you provide.

The first step is identifying these key terms. This involves understanding your audience—what they're searching for, the language they're using, and the kind of content they consume. Tools such as Google Keyword Planner or SEMrush offer invaluable data about keyword popularity and competition.

Once you've identified your vital keywords, they need to be seamlessly integrated into your content. However, be mindful of the catch: Overdone keyword integration, known as keyword stuffing, can lead to your site being marked as spam by search engines.

7.3. On-Page and Off-Page SEO

SEO consists of two complementary components—on-page and off-page SEO.

On-page SEO deals with optimizing elements of your own site. This includes but is not limited to:

- Content Quality: Original, engaging, and high-quality content is paramount.

- HTML Clues: Your meta tags, title tags, and headers should be properly formatted and include keywords where appropriate.

- Site Architecture: A clear, logical structure with a clean URL structure, efficient load times, and a responsive design is important.

Off-page SEO, on the other hand, involves external factors that you don't necessarily control but can influence. These include:

- Backlinks: These are external links on other sites that point to your webpage. The quantity and quality of backlinks lend credibility and authority to your site in the eyes of search engines.

- Social Sharing: The more your content is shared across social platforms, the better visibility you have, which indirectly benefits your SEO.

- Online Reputation: Your brand reputation plays a key role in your rankings. Garner positive reviews and navigate negative ones effectively.

7.4. Powerful SEO Tools to Utilize

Leveraging the correct tools can sharpen your SEO efforts. For keyword research, tools like Google Keyword Planner, SEMrush, and Ahrefs can provide valuable insights. Tools like Moz and Yoast SEO can help with optimizing your site structure and content. Google Analytics and Search Console offer powerful data about your site's performance and visitor behavior.

7.5. Implementing a Content Strategy

For effective SEO, consistent and high-quality content publication is crucial. A well-planned content strategy can exponentially increase your visibility. Regular blogging or article publication on topics related to your personal brand and keywords can boost your SEO.

7.6. Staying Abreast of SEO Changes

SEO is not a one-off endeavor but a constantly changing landscape. It's important to keep up with the latest updates in SEO algorithms and best practices. Subscribing to SEO blogs like Moz, Search Engine Journal, or Google Webmaster Central Blog can help you stay updated.

Mastering the science of SEO is a key factor in personal brand brilliance. Owning your online presence and optimizing it for maximum visibility will ensure that you stand out in the digital age.

Remember, SEO isn't just about visibility—it's about providing valuable content that resonates with your audience and builds brand credibility.

Chapter 8. The Impact of Authenticity in Digital Branding

In the digital age, authenticity is not just a buzzword; it's a cornerstone of successful personal branding. It's the ingredient that can set you apart from the sea of sameness in the online world. The explosion of social media platforms and the proliferation of digitally savvy users have created an insatiable demand for authentic interactions. As such, understanding the impact of authenticity in digital branding has never been more crucial.

8.1. The Nexus of Authenticity and Personal Branding

What is authenticity in a personal brand? It is a representation of an individual's true self, their beliefs, values, and personality, in a public, digital format. It's your distinct digital fingerprint. Being real on the internet isn't as easy as it seems, however. With the freedom digital platforms provide for individuals to project any image they desire, keeping one's true self intact requires discipline and intentionality.

Authenticity doesn't involve sharing every aspect of one's life online. However, it does mean refusing to project a manufactured, counterfeit, or exaggerated digital persona. An authentic personal brand leads to credibility and trust, which are both significant factors in building a sustainable online following. Thus, authenticity paves the way for influence and impact, unveiling opportunities that might be otherwise inaccessible.

8.2. The Influence of Authenticity on Audience Loyalty

Engagement in the digital sphere is significantly boosted when users perceive that they are interacting with a genuine personality. In fact, a study by the Boston Consulting Group (BCG) revealed that authenticity is one of the top qualities that would attract consumers to a brand. The underlying reason is quite instinctive: authenticity fosters trust and reliability.

An authentic brand is viewed as 'relatable', leading followers to feel a sense of kinship. This shared understanding elicits loyalty and positive word-of-mouth referrals, fueling the expansion of your digital presence.

8.3. The Role of Authenticity in Creating Unique Content

The digital market is saturated with sameness. A major part of authenticity is the courage to be unique, to voice out one's opinion and shine light on perspectives that are uniquely your own. Nothing separates your brand from a crowd of similar offerings better than leveraging authenticity to create exclusive and unique content. A truly authentic personal brand uses its unique selling proposition (USP) to share a distinct set of experiences with users.

8.4. Authenticity as a Growth Catalyst

In the digital world, where trends shift in an instant and today's innovations become tomorrow's old news, authenticity stands as a lasting, unshifting asset. Embracing authenticity boosts confidence in your own perspectives and fuel creativity, ultimately leading to growth. Beyond this, an honest brand persona attracts collaborations and partnerships with entities that recognise and appreciate your genuineness, leading to more opportunities for growth.

8.5. Overcoming the Pitfalls of Inauthenticity

The repercussions of inauthenticity can be severe. Negative reviews, dwindling follower count, and erosion of personal reputation are just some of the repercussions brands face when they abandon authenticity. Uncovering the ill effects of inauthentic practices such as 'clickbaiting' and 'faking testimonials' dramatically underscores the need to find and maintain a genuine brand personality.

8.6. Practical Steps to Nurtify Authenticity

Just as a diamond is formed over time, under pressure, an authentic personal brand isn't created overnight. It requires you to know your core values, align your brand with them and then remain consistent. Other actionable steps include embracing your uniqueness, telling personal stories, seeking and giving genuine feedback, showing vulnerability and, ultimately, being patient with your personal brand journey.

In conclusion, authenticity in branding creates a strong base from which to build a thriving digital persona. Remember, your unique factor isn't every other thing you share with the crowd - it's what sets you apart. By embracing and projecting that unique trait on your digital platform, you create a memorable and influential personal brand that radiates throughout the digital landscape.

Chapter 9. From Presence to Influence: Growing Your Brand Online

In the age of digital proliferation, establishing a robust online presence is only half of the journey. The true power lies in influencing, in imprinting one's personal brand on the hearts and minds of the people who encounter it. This chapter dives deeper into transforming your digital self-expression from mere presence to powerful influencer.

9.1. Cultivating a Strong Foundation

Remember that your online presence is an extension of who you are or, sometimes more importantly, who you want the world to perceive you as. It should not be a point of contention but rather a consistent stream that adapts to your evolving brand. Be it a LinkedIn profile, a personal website, a blog, or social media accounts, your voice, personality, and message should shine through harmoniously.

1. **Know Your Brand**: Eloquent expression of your personal brand requires self-awareness and clarity about who you are, what you represent, and how you want to be seen. This introspection lays the groundwork for your digital persona.

2. **Determine Your Audience**: Apart from clear self-identification, comprehension of your target audience is equally paramount. Knowing their needs, wants, aspirations and dilemmas allows you to generate content that resonates profoundly with them.

3. **Find Your Unique Value Proposition**: What sets you apart in this digital ocean is your Unique Value Proposition (UVP). Your UVP acts as a lighthouse, enabling you to stand out from the crowd and draw your audience to your content.

9.2. Harnessing the Power of Content

Creating content is a critical means to communicate your persona and ideals. It should fulfill a purpose, be it education, entertainment, inspiration, or sparking conversation.

1. **Quality Over Quantity**: Do not get overwhelmed with numbers. It's far more resourceful to share less frequently but more meaningfully than to constantly churn out mediocre content.

2. **Diverse Content for Diverse Platforms**: Differentiate your content based on the platforms. For example, LinkedIn is professional-centric, Instagram is visual-heavy, and Twitter is conversation-driven. Tailor your content accordingly but maintain the consistency of your personal brand expression.

3. **Consistent Engagement**: The key step towards influence is engaging with your audience. Respond to comments on your content, actively participate in relevant discussions, and show genuine interest in your community's opinions.

9.3. Building Thought Leadership

To substantialize your influence, positioning yourself as a thought leader is a powerful approach. This not only amplifies your voice but broadens your reach to potential followers and collaborators.

1. **Add Value**: Deliver more than just an opinion. Transform your content into valuable resources for your audience, offering insights, solutions, learning resources, or even motivation.

2. **Collaborate and Connect:** Connect with other influencers, engage with them, and collaborate on projects. This association can influence their audience's perception of you and open up new avenues to enhance your digital presence.

3. **Show Up Consistently**: Consistent exposure accents your credibility. Attend industry events, webinars, and engage in relevant online communities. Use these platforms to discuss and share your ideas.

4. **Leverage Media Attention**: Take opportunities to speak at conferences, write guest blog posts, or give interviews. Media attention can significantly boost your reputation and reach.

9.4. Navigating the Landscape of Social Media

Having complete control of your narrative on social media can significantly amplify your influence.

1. **Balance Personal and Professional Life**: As much as being authentic is celebrated, it's also crucial to maintain a balance between personal and professional aspects. Decide what to share and keep the rest to yourself.

2. **Adapt with the Changes**: With social media constantly evolving, staying updated with the latest trends is key. This flexibility enables your brand to remain consistent yet fresh.

3. **Engage in Social Listening**: Pay attention to the discussions happening around your brand or your professional field. This can provide invaluable insights to shape your personal brand and content strategy.

Lastly, remember the words of American author and speaker Simon Sinek, "People don't buy what you do; they buy why you do it." Your personal brand is your 'why', and this is what intrigues people, makes you relatable and eventually turns your online presence into influence.

In the next chapter, we'll investigate the nuances of dealing with challenges and obstacles in building a personal brand, and how to tackle criticism while staying true to your vision and maintaining your influence.

Chapter 10. Navigating Privacy in the Age of Personal Branding

The realm of personal branding, especially in the digital age, comes hand in hand with the ever-evolving concern of privacy. Balancing these two elements skillfully isn't just a boon, but in most cases, a crucial requirement. It involves understanding the thin line between what is enough to engage and effectively communicate with your audience, against what may jeopardize your personal privacy and safety.

10.1. Understanding the Importance of Privacy

The digital space is an open arena, where information, if made public, becomes visible to everyone - the good, the indifferent, and the malicious. This makes it crucial to appreciate the importance of privacy in personal branding. On the one hand, establishing a personal brand requires visibility and disclosure of certain personal information. On the other, protecting one's privacy necessitates the right regulations to keep certain data confidential. Striking the ideal balance calls for understanding the width of information to disclose and having a strategy to secure the rest.

Consider privacy as a part of your brand, something that offers value to you and your audience. When you carefully manage what information is available, it provides an opportunity to control your brand's narrative.

10.2. Creating a Privacy-Conscious Personal Brand

Building a personal brand involves making conscious decisions about what information to disclose. Disclosing relevant personal information – such as your expertise, experiences, and values – can build authenticity and trust with your audience. However, oversharing personal details can make you vulnerable.

Any information disseminated online, even if later deleted, could potentially exist permanently. Hence, it's vital that you cultivate thoughtful sharing habits. Examine each piece of information before posting, and only share what is essential for developing and maintaining your personal brand.

Adopt privacy settings across various platforms, especially in social media, where your interactions are mostly unfiltered. Also, regularly audit your public information to ensure its relevance and safety.

10.3. Dealing with Data Security

While you handle your disclosed information, remember that digital platforms are also repositories of your data. From subscription services that require your email to social platforms that analyze your likes and behavior, your data is constantly at work – often, without your active cognizance.

To ensure your data is not misused, familiarize yourself with the data policies of each platform you use. Adjust your privacy settings accordingly and use data protection measures like two-factor authentication, strong unique passwords, and secure personal networks.

Another significant aspect of data security is GDPR, especially if you or your audience are based in Europe. Be transparent with any data you may be collecting through your website, such as through newsletter sign-ups or cookies, and ensure GDPR compliance.

10.4. Responding to Breaches: What to Do When Your Privacy is Compromised?

Even after taking all the precautions, you might face breaches of privacy. You should have a prepared action plan for such incidents. First, identify the breach and assess its seriousness. If it involves any financial aspects, notify your bank and credit card companies immediately. Change your passwords, inform your followers if they could also possibly be affected, and take necessary legal action.

=== Maintaining a Proactive Privacy Approach

Successful navigation of privacy in personal branding is a continual process, not a one-time task. Implement the habit of routine privacy check-ups where you assess what information is publicly available. Stay updated with changes in data protection laws and social media privacy policies. Encourage your audience to do the same, which not only shows you respect their privacy but also helps in building trust.

The age of digital personal branding necessitates not just strategic expression but also conscious restriction. By respecting privacy – both yours and your audiences – while maneuvering through your personal branding journey, you invite a safer and more reliable digital environment for you and your followers.

Chapter 11. The Future of Personal Branding: Trends & Challenges Ahead

Understanding the future of personal branding involves more than a passing familiarity with trending hashtags, popular social media platforms, or knowing how to create a viral video—although these things can be beneficial. It's about predicting changes in technology, society, and user behaviors, and understanding the challenges that lie ahead to proactively manage and align our personal brands to these upcoming changes.

11.1. Decoding Future Trends

As we usher into the era of immersive technology and high-speed internet connection, the way we express our personal brands is set to undergo several substantial changes. The canvas of personal branding will continue to evolve, becoming more personalized, more authentic, more immersive, and boundlessly creative.

Let's take a look into the crystal ball and explore some of the key future trends that will shape the personal branding landscape.

1. **Hyper-Personalization**: Customization has always been integral to personal branding. However, with the vast amount of data available at their fingerprints, brands will be able to target their audience at a highly personalized level. From tailored content that resonates with individual beliefs, preferences, and interests, to personalized interfaces and customer experiences - hyper-personalization will be a significant trend.

2. **Authenticity Over Perfection**: The era of perfectly curated feeds with posed pictures and flawless aesthetics may very well be

over. There's a growing demand for authenticity, transparency, and imperfection, which makes personal brands relatable and human.

3. **Video Continues Its Reign**: The popularity of video content (reels, bites, live streaming, webinars, etc.) will continue to rise, owing to its high engagement rates and effectiveness in storytelling. Platforms like Instagram, TikTok, and YouTube are constantly developing features to leverage this trend.

4. **Voice and Audio Platforms**: While video content gains momentum, a new player enters the field – voice and audio-based content. Podcasts, audio blogs, and voice-based social networks like Clubhouse are rapidly growing arenas of personal branding.

5. **AI and Personal Branding**: As AI becomes more sophisticated, it will play a larger role in personal branding. Brands could employ AI tools to analyze trends, predict consumer behavior, and refine their strategies.

6. **Immersive Experiences**: Virtual Reality (VR) and Augmented Reality (AR) will emerge as new powerful tools in the pursuit of immersive personal branding. They can create unique experiences that engage the audience more intensely and meaningfully.

11.2. Challenges Ahead

Despite the exciting opportunities, the future landscape of personal branding doesn't come without its share of challenges.

Security and privacy remain significant concerns. The massive data collection used for hyper-personalization strategies raises important questions about privacy and data security. In the race to provide more personalized content, brands must ensure they're not crossing the line – and consumers grow increasingly vigilant.

Another challenge lies in mastering new skills needed to ride the wave of change. With AI, AR, and VR rapidly becoming essential parts of branding strategies, the need to understand and manage these technologies is more pressing than ever.

Then there's the competition. As more people get comfortable with personal branding, the online space is becoming increasingly crowded. Standing out and remaining top-of-mind will require more creativity, more authenticity, and more strategic thinking.

Lastly, balancing authenticity and professionalism can be tricky. Today's trend of demonstrating authenticity and transparency can blur the boundaries between personal and professional lives. Brands will need to tread carefully, ensuring that their authenticity does not compromise their professionalism.

11.3. Embracing the Future: In Conclusion

The future of personal branding is a blend of excitement and challenge, teeming with opportunities for those willing to adapt and evolve. It's about finding the balance between authenticity and professionalism, between personalization and privacy, and among the myriad platforms vying for your attention.

Regardless of the changes though, one fact remains unchanged: personal branding is about telling your story. No matter the medium, the trend, or the technology, the key to successful personal branding will always lie in the power of your narrative.

It's a horizon wide open. So, buckle up, because the digital landscape ahead will be nothing short of a rollercoaster ride, and the adventure to personal brand brilliance lies right before us.